An Instant out of Time

poems by

Gail Peck

Finishing Line Press
Georgetown, Kentucky

An Instant out of Time

ACKNOWLEDGMENTS

Grateful acknowledgment is made to the editors of the following
publications in which these poems first appeared:

Ekphrastic Review: "Eighty-year-old Woman Living in Squatter's Camp,
Bakersfield, California"; "Migrant Worker on California Highway"
Dead Mule School of Southern Literature: "Young Cotton Picker, Kern
County Migrant Camp, California"; "Fifty-seven-year-old Sharecropper
Woman. Hinds County, Mississippi"; "Pea Picker's Tent, Near Calipatria,
California"
Main Street Rag: "Tractored Out, Childress County, Texas"
Willawaw Journal: "Damaged Child, Shacktown, Elm Grove, Oklahoma"

I wish to thank Barbara Conrad, Rebecca McClanahan, Diana Pinckney and
Dede Wilson for their invaluable contributions to this manuscript. And my
gratitude to my steadfast husband, Jimmy Peck.

Publisher: Leah Maines
Editor: Christen Kincaid
Cover Art: Dorothea Lange
Author Photo: James Peck
Cover Design: Elizabeth Maines McCleavy

Printed in the USA on acid-free paper.
Order online: www.finishinglinepress.com
          also available on amazon.com

Author inquiries and mail orders:
Finishing Line Press
P. O. Box 1626
Georgetown, Kentucky 40324
U. S. A.

Table of Contents

Tractored Out, Childress County, Texas 1

Hitchhiking Family, Macon, Georgia 2

Migrant Mother, Nipoma, California 3

Young Cotton Picker, Kern County Migrant Camp, California..... 4

Damaged Child, Shacktown, Elm Grove, Oklahoma 5

Migrant Worker on California Highway 6

Washing Facilities on a Green County Georgia Tenant Farm 7

Fifty-seven-year-old Sharecropper Woman. Hinds County
    Mississippi 8

Mexican Children Playing in a Ditch. Corcoran, California.......... 9

Sick Migrant Child, Washington, Yakima Valley, Toppenish 10

Resettled Farm Child from Taos Junction to Bosque Farms
    Project, New Mexico 11

Wife of Tobacco Sharecropper in Kitchen of Home. Person
    County, North Carolina.. 12

Date Picker's Home. Coachella Valley, California........................ 13

Mother and Baby of Family on the Road. Tulelake, Siskiyou
    County, California... 14

Old Time Negro Living on Cotton Patch Near Vicksburg,
    Mississippi 15

The Only Home of a Depression-routed Family of Nine from
    Iowa 16

Carrot Pullers in Coachella Valley, California............................... 17

Migrants from Delaware Picking Berries in Southern New
    Jersey 18

Sharecroppers' Families Gathering Needs for Their 4th of July
    Celebration, Whites and Blacks Together. Hill House,
    Mississippi 19

Mother and Child, Yakima Valley, Near Wapato 20

Mexican Migratory Laborer.. 21

Eighty-year-old Woman Living in Squatter's Camp,
    Bakersfield, California 22

The House Trailer and the Youngest Little Girl. Washington,
    Yakima Valley, Toppenish.. 23

Peapicker's Tent, Near Calipatria, California................................ 24

Ma Burnham, Conway, Arkansas.. 25

Cotton Picker, Southern San Joaquin Valley, California............... 26

Corner of Kitchen. Home of Tobacco Sharecropper. Person
    County, North Carolina.. 27

Migrant Child in Shafter Camp, Farm Security Administration,
    California... 28

for
The Migrant Workers

Photography takes an instant out of time,
altering life by holding it still.
Dorothea Lange

Preface

Dorothea Lange accepted a job with the Resettlement Administration in 1935, later known as the FSA, Farm Security Administration. Her photographs were intended to bolster support for the establishment of migrant camps in the Imperial Valley. Migrants were arriving from the Midwest to California as many as six thousand a month, "driven by unemployment, drought, and the loss of farm tenancy." Lange documented the living conditions, makeshift camps and the extreme poverty occurring at the time of the Great Depression and the Dust Bowl.

Dorothea Lange wrote of the people she was photographing:

> *Their roots were all torn out. The only background they had was a background of poverty. It's very hard to photograph a proud man against a background like that, because it doesn't show what he's proud about. I had to get my camera to register the things about those people that were more important than how poor they were— their pride, their strength, their spirit.*

Tractored Out, Childress County, Texas

Set in the midst of furrows.
A small house. No smoke from the chimney,
no people. They tried to hold on.
Oh, yes, next year's crop will yield,
and the dust will cease.
One child after another,
Dust Pneumonia threatening death.
Finally, the people moved on to Oklahoma
where conditions were the same,
then to California: *No Oakies Allowed.*
Now the fields are silent,
no sound of tractors.
The price of wheat falling and falling.
What might be left inside the house?
What wasn't necessary,
wouldn't fit in the jalopy.
The straight, flat road ahead.
Signs to count the miles.
Stories for the children
to ward off hunger.
The mother saying, *Soon.*

Hitchhiking Family, Macon, Georgia

There is nothing to do but wait.
All except the father sit
beside the road. He seems resigned
to whatever fate. What they own
in suitcases and boxes. The daughter
wears a light-colored hat like her mother,
a dress made from the same fabric.
Two brothers nearby.

The father had repaired sewing machines
and lawnmowers, but did not have
twenty-five dollars required
for the license in Georgia,
so was returning to Alabama.
The telephone poles and wires
stretch overhead. Who will pick them up,
and will they take them far?
Dust after each passing car.
The questions of the children,
waved away like insects in the grass.

Migrant Mother, Nipoma, California

She's thirty-two but the lines in her forehead
make her look much older. She holds the nursing baby
who won't go hungry. Two of her other children,
with their hair cropped, rest on each side of her shoulders,
their faces turned away. Whatever she's thinking
seems inward, her right hand at her chin which she
tugs slightly down. There are four more children
we do not see here. She sold her tent and the tires
to her car to buy food, and lives beneath
a makeshift shelter. She'd come to this part of California
to pick peas and discovered
they were destroyed by freezing rain.
They are eating vegetables that have frozen
in nearby fields, birds the children kill.
Her mother had told her she'd made her bed
and to lie in it. What young woman
listens to their mother? Her husband
had laid his weight on her, again and again, not caring
if the children heard. Now, she gathers
the small ones to her when night comes.

Young Cotton Picker, Kern County Migrant Camp, California

What is she waiting for, standing
in the dirt with no one around?
As if she held all the weight
in the world, this girl with a cotton sack
several feet long.
She looks to be eight or nine,
eyes closed beneath her blonde bangs.
She leans her head on one hand.
In the background, the camp
and a jalopy. This child
should be at play or school,
learning to read and write.
Awakened before dawn
when the moon still shone
on the dew. She will soon
remove her coat, but will cling
to the sack, the way other children
might hold a blanket
they won't surrender.

Damaged Child, Shacktown, Elm Grove, Oklahoma

She stands before a shelter of patched tin,
in a sack-like sleeveless dress
tied at one shoulder. The dress is soiled,
mere covering. All that she's seen
caught in her stare, lips pursed
as if defying the camera. Her hair is short
and parted and pushed behind
her ears so that none falls on her face.

The only casual thing about her is how loosely
her hands slide halfway into her pockets.
A hint of breasts. When she begins to menstruate,
her mother will tear cloth for pads, and warn her
of all that can happen living in such a place,
men coming and going. The mother's worries,
now more than food and medicine.
Days are long, there's nothing beautiful here
except the sunset.

What is this child's name?
Perhaps Lillian or Margaret,
something suited to her stance.
In another photograph, she is barefoot.
When winter comes there might be a pair of boots
already pinching her toes, but she will not cry.
She will not.

Migrant Worker on California Highway

Caught in mid-step with many more
to go. A hat to shade him from the sun.
This man is carrying everything
he owns over his left shoulder.
Soon he will shift the bundle
to the other shoulder.
Dust settles on his clothes, his face,
in his nose. Only a worn handkerchief
in his back pocket to wipe away sweat.
Perhaps a car will come by, but they are usually
laden with belongings and numerous children.
He's getting hunched from bending to crops,
longs for the reach of apples and peaches,
the shade of the trees. He doesn't mind lying
beneath the stars, the sounds of the insects.
He'll sleep from exhaustion,
and dream. It is then the lost ones
will return, picking up in mid-sentence.

Washing Facilities on a Green County Georgia Tenant Farm

At the side of a clapboard house
raised on brick pillars, a woman
bends to the wash tub. The tub
is balanced on a straight-back chair.
She wears a straw hat, her sleeves
are rolled up with her hands in the water.
How far did she carry the water?

My grandmother washed on a board,
metal framed by wood to earn food
for my mother and herself.
When she got a ringer machine,
she let me help as the clothes went through.

Perhaps, in this house, the woman
has beans cooking on the stove,
soaked the night before.
It is summer and there might be peaches.
How good they will taste after she takes off
her shoes and sits in a cane chair. The cane is broken,
but she isn't used to comfort.
Her stomach will be full,
and that's something.

Fifty-seven-year-old Sharecropper Woman. Hinds County Mississippi

When there are no doctors
you do what you can, a dime with a hole
on a string tied around each ankle
to prevent headaches.
Her bare feet rest on the planks
of a porch, her feet so calloused
it's hard to feel splinters.
How many miles have they walked among rows?
Her hand touches the hem
of her dress covered with a soiled apron.
Past child-bearing, she holds her grandchildren
to her, on her lap. If only the headaches
would cease. All her prayers to make them stop
have yet gone unanswered.
Surely, the Good Lord can be trusted,
yet she's seen so much misery, so much hunger.
Still, she washes as best she can on Sunday
to walk to church. She has no hat, no purse,
and carries a few coins when she can get them
inside a cloth bag, and places one or two
into the plate, small offering to God.

Mexican Children Playing in a Ditch. Corcoran, California

Imagination is all they need,
a ditch filled with water,
two small boys on one side,
a young girl on the other.
She's rapt in whatever
they are examining or building.
You can't see the boys' faces.
One has long hair
and is bending in front of the other.
This a moment without bickering.
The land usually dry has left
a lake, a lagoon, some sticks
for building a moat for protection.

Sick Migrant Child, Washington, Yakima Valley, Toppenish

You can sense the nausea by her expression.
She lies on a board on the ground,
propped on two pillows, in overalls,
no shirt underneath. Beside her is a beat-up cup.
Her elbow is resting on the board,
and her hand over her chest.
How long can she stay there
before having to move on to the next crop?
At night, where does she sleep,
and what is her bed like?
She could grow to be beautiful.
Now there is the dirt that gets under her fingernails,
on her face, her feet. Those around her
are hungry, and seldom smile,
same clothes worn day after day,
dirty and threadbare. No money
for medicine, so they drink tea
made from roots. This girl's parents
must be in the fields, her mother
wanting desperately to be with her,
helping to lift her head to drink.

Resettled Farm Child from Taos Junction to Bosque Farms Project, New Mexico

If there were a book, she'd read it.
If there were a record, she'd play it.
One bench where she sits
near a rusted iron bed. She stares at the fireplace.
At least this is shelter from the dust, though it seeps
through the cracks, down the chimney.
You can hear the rattle of wind.

Today, sun shines on her dress.
I want to think it's the same color as the sun.
Twelve, thirteen? She wears sturdy shoes,
her most prized possession, across the sod floor.
Where is her family—in the fields?

I moved many times.
My father, who was in the army,
would come home and say
we'd be packing soon.
We'd travel in the car, my mother
in front, my sisters beside me.
I dreamed of a house with shutters
and a front porch, but it was always army quarters.

What happened to this nameless girl
as lovely as a painting, her face
leaning against one hand.
What is she thinking?

Wife of Tobacco Sharecropper in Kitchen of Home. Person County, North Carolina

The glass kerosene lamp
may be the most decorative thing
this family owns. The mother is cleaning
the oilcloth spread over the table where a few dishes
rest, some spoons in a jar. At the screen door,
a young girl about three stands in the light.
She's come in for something to eat,
water from the dipper.
I taste the metal of the dipper's rim.
She's pretty, and fairly clean
for having played in dirt. What does
the mother have to feed her? Her own figure
is ample, so there must be food,
even if it must last—a biscuit with jam
that was canned in summer.

This child is the "knee baby,"
second to the youngest. Maybe the mother
will place a bowl of applesauce on the table.
I can feel that waxy cloth
of my childhood, something colorful with design.
Then the child will return to play outside:
sticks for people, leaves for shelter.

Date Picker's Home. Coachella Valley, California

No one would call this
Home Sweet Home—
tin patched together,
straw at one end.
A young boy and girl,
or is it two girls,
stand in the doorway,
the floor inside no different
from the outside.
This place without windows,
set in the valley.
Coachella, originally Conchilla—
little shell for fossils
found in the area.
What a shell of a home
for these two urchins,
the soles of their feet
impossible to get clean.
Everything is makeshift.
Soon they will move on
to orchards of grapefruit,
lemons. The parents
probably picking dates.
We see only the children,
for this moment,
not asking for a thing.

Mother and Baby of Family on the Road, Tulelake, Siskiyou, California

The mother sits in the car wearing a coat
with a fur collar, holding a child
whose clothes and face
are dirty. Propped against the child
is a Coke bottle with a nipple.
The child's eyes are as questioning
as the mother's eyes behind round glasses.
There's a blanket around her, next to her blonde hair.
The mother's lips are parted,
perhaps longing to say something of regret
for what was left behind.
It wasn't much of a house,
and crops failed due to the Dust Bowl,
but there were curtains at the window,
a table for meals. Now her husband leans
against the back of the car, smoking.
He seems to be looking at nothing,
one hand in his jacket pocket
as if there were all the time in the world.

Old Time Negro Living on Cotton Patch Near Vicksburg, Mississippi

His back is to us,
his left hand holding
sharp-tipped weeds
as he stands along
the roadside.
Suspenders hold up his pants,
and he wears a hat
with a band.
I've never seen a shirt
so ragged, a bit of cover
from the sun.
I must imagine his face
that might tell me his age.
Is there even a dollar
in his pants pocket.
If so, he'd guard it.
These are hard times
in Mississippi—a state
my grandmother taught me
to spell. I want to say,
Turn around, but his man
doesn't want me to see
his face. So, he stands
staring off, maybe thinking
of resting in the shade,
of folding his calloused hands
one over the other.

The Only Home of a Depression-routed Family of Nine from Iowa

They are shirtless, these two small boys
in overalls who stand at the back
of a trailer hitched to a car while the mother
adjusts something on top.
The family, on their way to Mexico,
is about to sell the trailer
and some of their belongings to buy food.
The second photograph of the car
shows clothes hanging from an open window.
At night they pull off the road,
haul down the mattress.
The father coughs, as he has TB,
the sick baby cries.
The boys wrestle, and they all fear
the dark, the sound of coyotes.
The mother tries to quiet them,
but they are hungry. If they can get enough money,
they'll buy gas too, fill the large can
with its narrow handle and spout.

Carrot Pullers in Coachella Valley, California

You must bend to the earth,
get your hands dirty,
grit under your nails.
Your knees will creak with age
and cause pain.
You'll wear long sleeves
as protection from the sun.
And wear your clothes
as long as you can
before washing them.

The crates for the carrots
stand blonde in the field
that seems to stretch forever.
Carrots with their feathery tops,
for soups and salads.
To think of the warm soup,
the salad with dressing, will make you hungry.

You have no home, one camp
following another where you speak
your own language, and roll paper
around tobacco, strike a match
then blow it out.

Migrants from Delaware Picking Berries in Southern New Jersey

One is deep
in the berry patch
while the other stands barefoot
in a dirt row. The berries
might be strawberries, blueberries
or gooseberries. Their work is slow
as they must ease the berries from the vine.
Suited for a woman's patience.
After laboring all day,
if the orchard owner gives them
berries to take home,
they will wash them, add sugar
and put the mixture
into crusts carefully rolled out.
The ovens will heat
as the liquid rises to the top.
If there's more than enough for the families,
neighbors may receive pies
after they have cooled. Pie covered
with cloth and carried by steady hands.
This is the sweetness that sustains.

Sharecroppers' Families Gathering Needs for Their 4th of July Celebration, Whites and Blacks Together. Hill House, Mississippi

All the children are barefoot,
two of the white girls hold melons,
a woman stands behind. The two black girls
wear hats, and one holds a box.
One white man, and one black man at the far left.

I don't know if the children have played together,
or if they will sit at the same table.
They are dressed nicely, and they all are clean,
except for the bottoms of their feet
that are used to stubble, the occasional bee.

Will they have fried chicken, biscuits?
Will the white hands touch the black?

The melons are still warm from the field,
the juice will be delicious—red of the watermelon,
orange of the cantaloupe.

Soon they will step from this platform
they are balanced on, and run about
as children do, playing tricks on one another.

For now, none of them smile.

Mother and Child, Yakima Valley, Near Wapato

You first notice the expression
on the young girl's face that is downcast,
her dark hair parted. Her hands curved around
the smooth places on the barbed wire fence.
What is it keeping in or out?
The girl is wearing a floral print dress
with a large, white collar which can't possibly
stay clean in that dust. Her mother in the background
is shielding her eyes from the sun.
You can't tell if there's a resemblance
to the child who may be looking at something
that escaped to the other side of the fence.
You want to ask, *A penny for your thoughts.*

Mexican Migratory Laborer

This man kneels on the earth
to thin and weed cantaloupes.
The young plants are capped
with wax paper over a wire wicket,
protection against cold.
This is Imperial, California—
imperial—of superior quality.
The cantaloupes are trucked to markets
and displayed, where the buyers can choose.
In restaurants, the staff will serve the cold
melon with vanilla ice cream on a china plate.
Restaurants this man has never entered.
He moves along the rows, a roll of wax paper
tucked in the back of his pants.
He'll tear the sheets, tent the melons
for thirty cents an hour. He can see his work
stretched before him, thirty-two inches apart,
little white domes.

Eighty-year-old Woman Living in Squatter's Camp, Bakersfield, California

Her hair has thinned, her round glasses
low on her nose. I doubt she has many teeth
the way her mouth is set. Yet, she has advice:
"If you lose your pluck you lose
the most that is in you."
She sits in a car. She is wearing a plaid dress
with cuffs and wide collar.
I would not want to tangle with her,
although the man beside her
probably has. He is in her shadow
and I didn't see him at first.
I think of a long marriage,
that he's learned to give in.

To live on the outskirts of town
in a shack of tin. What do the wrinkles
in this woman's face reveal—
the death of a child,
illness or the constant counting of change
for bread and milk.
She has one hand on her forehead
shielding her eyes from the sun.
She wants to see clearly what is before her.

The House Trailer and the Youngest Little Girl. Washington, Yakima Valley, Toppenish

The door is flung open,
and she leans in the doorway
looking out at what I don't know.
Better to have this house than none,
even if everyone is cramped inside—
beds that fold down from the wall,
and a table too. A portable home.

I lived in a trailer as a child,
fascinated by the smallness,
and how we had to move around
one another. You could see inside
the other trailers' windows.

I never knew the words *Trailer Trash*.
I played with the other kids, running
between the small lots. When my family
moved, it was to a bigger trailer.

This young girl doesn't know
she's looking at the future,
all that is outside this door.
There's Mt. Rainier, often obscured
by clouds, with snow on top.
She may long for a house
like the ones she passes
in the car, houses with mailboxes nearby
and porches where people sit.

Pea Pickers's Tent, Near Calipatria, California

Someone with a sense of humor
   has plopped a man's hat
on top of this ragged tent.

A washboard leans against it,
   and there's an upside-down basket
with a metal pan.

The flap of the opening
   is pulled back, but all
you can see is darkness.

At least it's protection
   from the sun, and if it does rain . . .
Come to think of it, let it storm,

let the wind carry the whole thing off,
   and tear it apart, let the pieces scatter,
a testament to all who are still

coming westward, passing the signs:
   No Jobs for Oakies, whose homes
will be shacks or a tent like this one.

Ma Burnham, Conway, Arkansas

How many women have I known
like this, wearing a print dress,
ankles swollen. She sits in a straight-back chair
on the porch. Her hands are clasped in her lap.
Behind her is a screen door, a window
with parted curtains. When I learn she's raised
twelve children, I know how little rest she's gotten—
only when stringing beans, shelling peas,
reading her Bible. Her expression is resolute,
her thin hair pushed behind her ears.
Her breasts sag. I imagine she has only a few
dresses, a couple for Sundays. A few pairs of shoes,
at least one pair for church. The stories she could tell us:

"My father was a Confederate soldier. He give his age
a year older than it was to get in the army. After the war
he bought 280 acres . . . Now, none of my children
own their own land."

Land: dirt to build a house on, dirt
to till to feed your family. The farm machinery
leased to the bank,
everyone praying for rain.

Cotton Picker, Southern San Joaquin Valley, California

She has a lovely smile,
perfect teeth. Her arms
are folded behind her back,
a long cotton sack is tied
around her waist.
She is Mexican,
and I wish I could see
the color of her dress.
What good news makes her smile,
or is it only for the camera?
Is it the end of a long day?
I like to think she'll soon
remove the cotton sack,
and there will be music,
and dance—her full skirt
flaring out like a tulip opening.

Corner of Kitchen. Home of Tobacco Sharecroppers.
Person County, North Carolina

A stove with a few pots. Wood stove
where you had to guess
at temperature, watch closely.

To the right is a butter churn.
To the left, a table with an oilcloth,
a large dishpan on top.

The smell of coffee
in the mornings when light
comes through the window.

Early morning before a day
in the fields—a year-round
chore of tilling, sowing, transplanting,
removing worms and suckers.

Then harvesting and drying the tobacco
before trucking it to market.
Then starting all over again.

The corner of the kitchen
where a woman cooks
and sets plates before her family,
fatback, gravy and biscuits.
On occasion, a slice of country ham.

Migrant Child in Shafter Camp, Farm Security Administration, California

He is the dirtiest, happiest towhead,
missing several front teeth. You can barely
make out that there are cartoon characters
on his sweatshirt—Porky Pig?
We're told he lives in a tent instead
of in a ditch bank. He must have played in mud,
his sleeves are soiled and would never come clean.
Does he have a secret hiding place?
I believe he'd never tell, not for a dime,
maybe a quarter. There is trust
in his smile. You want to slip a clean shirt
over his head. Foolish you.
Dirt calls to him.

Gail Peck holds an M.F.A. from Warren Wilson College. Her first chapbook won the North Carolina Harperprints Award, and her first full-length won the *Texas Review* Breakthrough Contest. *Main Street Rag* published her chapbook *Foreshadow* (a finalist) and two full-length books, *Thirst* and *Counting the Lost*. Other chapbooks include *From Terezin* (Pudding House) and *Within Two Rooms* (Finishing Line Press). Her collection, *The Braided Light* won the 2014 Lean Shull Book Contest. Poems and essays have appeared in *The Southern Review, Nimrod, Greensboro Review, Louisville Review, Comstock Review, Mississippi Review, Rattle, Connotation Press, Brevity, Cave Wall* and elsewhere. Peck's work has been widely anthologized, and she has been both a finalist and semi-finalist for *Nimrod*'s Pablo Neruda Prize for Poetry. Her poetry and essays have appeared in numerous anthologies and has been nominated for a Pushcart Prize and Best of the Net. Her essay, "Child, Waiting," was cited as notable by *Best American Essays*, 2013.

www.ingramcontent.com/pod-product-compliance
Lightning Source LLC
LaVergne TN
LVHW051610080426
835510LV00020B/3222